IN THE
GARDEN
ROY
GENDERS

MEADOW MANOR

RACHEL ASHWELL'S

MEADOW MANOR

MY MAJESTIC ENGLISH COUNTRYSIDE HOME

PHOTOGRAPHY BY AMY NEUNSINGER

CICO BOOKS

Photographer: Amy Neunsinger

Text: Rachel Ashwell and
Alexandra Parsons

Index: Hilary Bird

Editor: Sophie Devlin

Designer: Geoff Borin

Senior commissioning editor: Annabel Morgan

Art director: Sally Powell

Creative director: Leslie Harrington

Head of production: Patricia Harrington

Published in 2026 by CICO Books
An imprint of Ryland Peters & Small Ltd
20–21 Jockey's Fields
London
WC1R 4BW

and

1452 Davis Bugg Road
Warrenton, NC 27589

www.rylandpeters.com
Email: euregulations@rylandpeters.com

10 9 8 7 6 5 4 3 2

A CIP record for this book is available from the British Library.

US Library of Congress CIP data has been applied for.

ISBN: 978 1 80065 569 0

The authorised representative in the EEA is Authorised Rep Compliance Ltd., Ground Floor, 71 Lower Baggot Street, Dublin, D01 P593, Ireland
www.arccompliance.com

Printed in China

CONTENTS

INTRODUCTION
MY SOULFUL SANCTUARY

A few years ago, I found my heart being drawn to spending more time in my homeland of England after four decades living in Los Angeles. I didn't fully think through how it might all work, given I have adult children and businesses in both places, and although I have never lost the feeling of being British, after all that time I also felt somewhat American. I decided not to get hung up on the "what-ifs" or needing all the answers, but to follow my heart where it was leading me and trust that all would make sense later. Maybe it would be forever, or just another chapter. Life, after all, is but a series of chapters.

My home in Los Angeles has many of the qualities of an English country home, with its spacious surroundings of ocean and canyons, so even though I had spent very little time in the English countryside, the prospect of having rolling, open green spaces where the seasons had time to express their presence became a priority over the idea of city life. I had no idea of what part of the English countryside to choose, as I grew up a London girl, but I had two country-dwelling friends, Pearl Lowe and Christina Strutt. With their encouragement and support, I decided to narrow my scope and focus on Somerset in England's south-west.

I initially rented a cottage on a sheep farm, where horses were also boarded. It was a good balance, as my cottage was tucked away and quiet, giving me time to gently observe how I was settling in far away from the life I had built in Los Angeles. All around me were the timeless activities of farm life, both the animals and the community that comes along with a working farm. I discovered the TV series *All Creatures Great and Small*, about a country vet in 1930s Yorkshire, which often mirrored the life I was beginning to live.

My rental cottage became a sanctuary for my heart and the perfect stepping stone to a new life, an anchor, as I searched for somewhere to buy while continuing to spend some months in Los Angeles. The movie *The Holiday* in parts reflected my reality. In the end, it took three years to find the home I eventually purchased—the complexities of the Covid pandemic made the competition and elevated costs of buying a home beyond challenging for a while. But the universe's hand in slowing down the process was fortuitous, as there were many aspects of country life that I learnt I needed to consider.

RIGHT *I love tufted velvet for seating, mushy and soft yet handsome and regal. This teal sofa is perfectly at home in a country manor or a rustic barn.*

My dream was to find a small house, with maybe three bedrooms, a little bit of land and garden and unobstructed views. But I soon learned that most of the smaller houses were in villages with little land to speak of, while the larger ones with the surroundings I was envisioning could be isolating. I didn't want a massive reconstruction project, just a decorative one. And majestic light was important to me, even though in reality the sunshine is elusive during the long winter months.

I found driving around the small country lanes very comforting, making room for horses, tractors or other cars as we all navigated passing spaces on roads barely wide enough for one vehicle. This was a beautiful sign to me of the simple joy I felt when experiencing the common values of patience, acceptance and humanity, which are not evident when driving the fast, aggressive freeways of Los Angeles.

As I continued my search—there were several nearly homes—I was mindful of the importance of my heart and soul taking on this change, noticing what was in alignment with my truth and what felt unfamiliar or uncomfortable. While in some ways I was returning home, 40 years is a long time and London was the place I left as a young teenager, where I hadn't yet built up a history or even knew much of who I was. Now I was exploring a new life for a me who had already lived a life with all its trials and tribulations. I had a lot of understanding of who I was, but I was stepping into a life where only I knew who I was. Moving out of our comfort zone makes room for growth, but there were moments of loneliness and uncertainty. I let myself sit in those moments.

In time, I crossed paths with Meadow Manor. My first experience of the house was walking through a wonky farm gate and across a lawn-laid garden leading to a glass-paned wooden door. A charming original brass doorbell operated by a string pulley was a good sign that this home retained some of its authentic details, which are so often replaced with soulless modern conveniences. I entered directly into the warm welcome of the kitchen, the working fireplace throwing out both emotional and physical warmth, along with an aroma from something yummy baking in the Aga stove. It was life from a storybook.

LEFT *My dog George and me on one of our escapades through the billowing grasses in the meadow. The landscape here rolls away as far as the eye can see.*

Buying Meadow Manor was a slow process, as the family I purchased it from had lived an idyllic life there for 30 years. While it was the right time for them to begin a new chapter, it was still an emotional decision for them to let go. We built up a relationship through the selling and buying process. The owners felt that we are all just custodians of these beautiful old homes, so it was important to them to pass their home to someone with similar values. They had a large extended family but were looking to downsize, which gave me cause to consider my need for a house of this size. In some ways, that question remains unanswered.

Meadow Manor is abundant with light. The house is surrounded with majestic vistas as well as an orchard, lawns and a walled garden. But it is within easy walking distance of my local pub and corner shop, and glimmers of light from neighboring properties give me the comfort of people nearby. The front of the house faces a road, but the passing traffic noise is mainly the clip-clop of horses or the low rumble of slow-moving tractors. It is Grade II listed, meaning the building, both inside and out, is protected by the local planning authority, who carefully monitor any maintenance or improvements to ensure that they are sympathetic to the origins and character of the house. It is thanks to these restrictions that Meadow Manor has retained its grace and serenity over 400 years.

I bought very few furnishings for my new/old manor, trusting that the leftover pieces from the different lives I had lived, including those from my beloved Texan B&B, The Prairie, would find their perfect space. I shipped over two containers of my treasures, trusting they would somehow flow together in a completely different setting. And of course they did. As long as something is beautiful, it will always fit in.

RIGHT *A well-lived-in room. I massively love my tiny snug with its Shabby Chic sofa, slipcover and sofa topper. The intimate proportions and eclectic palette of florals and patina are rich and welcoming, whether just for me or for friends and family.*

OVERLEAF *England's rich architectural heritage is largely shaped by the diverse types of stone used in buildings. These materials typically reflect the local geology, giving each town and village a unique character. I love the honey-colored Doultingstone of Meadow Manor, with all its imperfections and evidence of age. It's a beautiful stone, solid and accountable for the Manor standing tall for hundreds of years. The double Roman tiled roof is another signature of the area that has stood the test of time. I find the symmetry of the structure and placement of the windows, along with the chimneys, simply divine. Picture-book perfect.*

CASA
VOGUE
n.31

THE GROUND FLOOR

THE HEARTBEAT OF THE HOUSE

When I first walked into the farmhouse, I could envisage what was eventually to become the heartbeat of the home. The ground floor is essentially that, a place where all activities come together in a beautiful symphony, embracing the kitchen, the dining room, my design room, the laundry and the living rooms. It is a creative space, welcoming a carousel of friends and family, with every room having its own meaningful, beautiful and peaceful function.

THE LIVING ROOM
A SPACE TO GATHER

My vision for this room was one of texture and raw materials offset with romantic twinkles from the chandeliers and the plush comfort of plentiful cushions. My first consideration was to set the stage and the color palette. The original red pinewood floors were stubborn and did not want to part ways with their orange tone, despite my attempts to strip, acid-wash and stain them. In the end, I let them rest in all their orange glory and covered them with reclaimed wide wood planks—shelving from a cheese factory—that were the perfect neutral tone.

I had planned to be braver with my paint selection in lieu of my signature white walls, but I quickly realized that given the combination of lime plaster walls and the dramatic influence of the seasonal British light, I would need more time, along with more courage, which I will revisit in time before introducing colors. Instead, I stayed in my comfort zone of shades of white, which proved to be enough of a challenge, as the shades bounced from creamy to gray. Even now, depending on the time of day or the season, my walls have a mind of their own.

The room is a rectangle with a fireplace at one end, so there wasn't a great deal of wiggle room when it came to deciding what pieces would go where. Creating a comfy and communal space for myself and my guests was my practical consideration. I truly love the big mushy Shabby Chic sofas I have been making for 40 years, with their practical machine-washable slipcovers. Two of those, along with an armchair, were all the room could accommodate in terms of seating. The floors are too glorious to need rugs, and other mismatched bits and pieces I thoughtfully placed to ground the room with a sense of artful shabbiness.

RIGHT *I wanted to create a space that was functional but not fussy. Installing reclaimed cheese boards as flooring, still with subtle stains where the round cheeses once rested, set the stage for all the cast of characters to follow. Overstuffed Shabby Chic sofas juxtaposed with a mid-century leather and chrome footstool are the anchors of the eclectic aesthetic. The vintage fire screen brings some humility to the rather fanciful fireplace. The petite chandelier is a tad disproportionate for the room, but I felt the chunky crystals compensate with their dynamic twinkles.*

OVERLEAF *The Shabby Chic white linen armchair is beautiful, comfortable and functional, as the covers are machine washable (left). These fading, fluffy roses are a portrait of romance to me (right).*

Best

LEFT *A cascading floral display, designed by Toria Britten, creates a spectacular poetic moment.* **ABOVE** *A snapshot of perfect imperfection: a Shabby Chic Belgian linen slipcover, forgiving of wear and always at its best when a little wavy and rumpled.* **OVERLEAF** *I painted this alcove in Francesca's Paints in Rose, diluted by 50%, to create a soothing backdrop for my collection of religious figurines (left). While I don't consider myself religious, I am drawn to the essence of motherly love; gentle and serene. As an ensemble, the figures make a peaceful yet profound statement. A contemplative bust is positioned quietly next to the glitter of glamorous crystals (right).*

London Interiors
TASCHEN
Jane Edwards
INTERIORS
MARC JACOBS
TELLER
STEIDL

LEFT *My forever-to-keep porcelain candlesticks have graced many pages in my previous books. They have gathered a few chips over the years, but although a little fragile nowadays, they retain their pretty poise.*

ABOVE *I painted the fireplace a clean matt white to offset the shabby vintage mirror and had some barely there flowers painted onto the panel to bring a teeny detail of charm: faded grandeur in reverse.*

THE SNUG
THE BIG LITTLE ROOM

I love this room. While its proportions are small, it can still handle substantial statements. The star of the show is the handsome blond fireplace, which could have commanded attention in a larger room. Here it sits proudly and protectively among its romantic and eclectic co-stars. The snug is my safe space to meditate, and often friends and family opt to snuggle together in this cosy, contained space in preference to the larger living room. I am drawn to this room for its nurturing and enveloping quality. It is where all floral affairs coexist in harmony, the essence of a lovely philosophy of life.

The long, dark and chilly days of country living led me to lessons in curtains, which back in California were mainly floaty voile panels thumbtacked casually in place. Window dressings, I am now learning, serve the function of warmth as well as influencing the decor of a room—quite an overwhelming subject, involving great expense, an array of fabric choices, linings, interlinings and hardware. I was relieved to repurpose drapes that had previously hung in a family room at The Prairie. Their rich, chintzy palette complemented the original dark-stained floorboards and the hardware. However, they were a tad too short, so I added some leftover sage green velvet to add length.

Initially I tested my courage and painted the walls a warm shade of teal. It was lovely, but just not me, at least not yet. So I repainted the lower third of the wall in a shade of pink that I diluted by 70%, barely noticeable until you see the join with the creamy paint above. I continued the hues of pink by layering a blush ombre damask rug on the dark wood floor. I love the combination of pinks and browns. The twinkly chandelier with pink drops was one of the few of my magical chandeliers to switch successfully from US to UK wiring codes, and there she hangs beautifully.

Another of my Shabby Chic sofas fits perfectly along the wall facing the fireplace. The slipcover and sofa topper layered with an abundance of cushions speaks to my mantra: beauty, comfort and function. All the fabrics are machine washable, which served me well when my kids had sandy feet in Malibu and even more so now with the muddy paws of country pups.

My mum would also have loved this room and her presence is felt here by way of her chair, slipcovered in a sun-bleached paisley print; ironically, she didn't much love floral fabrics. The slipcover is threadbare on the arms, which I love as evidence of where her gentle hands lay—a meaningful moment for me.

RIGHT *Often I move things from room to room, for photo shoots or to see how new designs look in situ. Sometimes they look so lovely on the move, I leave them as an impermanent moment.*

OVERLEAF *My beloved snug is home to a symphony of florals in different tones, some quiet and faded, some bold and commanding. I purposely chose a striped slipcover to complement the array of florals. Although the slipcover is machine washable, the ruffled floral sofa topper in Shabby Chic Rose Blossom Teal gives an additional layer of protection from sticky hands and muddy paws. As with most of the furnishings of Meadow Manor, these are hand-me-downs from other lives I have lived. The Sanderson curtains had been packed away for years since The Prairie, waiting for the perfect spot.*

ROMANCE

ABOVE *Beautiful Bennison Rosevine is a pattern I have loved forever. I have a sense of pride when I see how my Shabby Chic Rose Blossom in Teal has a sense of belonging with this exquisite fabric.*
RIGHT *The Charnwood wood burner in the fireplace gives me all the romance of a fire without the fuss.*

OVERLEAF *Magical moments with flowers and art. The watercolors—I call them Raspberry Girls—are by Jorunn Mulen (left). I enjoy their whimsy displayed on the coffee table. My local friend Victoria Sheppard, an artisan grower, supplied this timeless rose bouquet of an assortment of David Austin varieties (right).*

TIM WALKER

HALLWAYS
THE UNSUNG HEROES

These are the well-trodden paths that greet us or take us on a journey from room to room. They are not places to linger or to ponder about, but they still deserve our consideration. There are two entrances to Meadow Manor: one is into the kitchen from the front garden, while the other is at the side of the house and accessed through the walled garden. I find that guests and deliveries use both equally, but the side entrance has no bell, so a loud knock is required.

Well-worn flagstone floors, beautiful to look at as well as a testament to generations of footfall, set the stage for a country home experience. I collected vintage Ushak rugs, largely from Etsy, to provide warmth here, both emotionally and practically. Inevitably mud is traipsed through this space, but a quick sweep and shake takes care of that, so there's no need to be precious. One thing I did learn about the English entrance hall was the need to keep out the wind and the cold. I have embraced the idea of the door curtain, drawn back in summer but deployed on a winter's night.

Meadow Manor was built in the 1600s, so it's hard to know exactly what was what at the beginning. But the thought is that the archway through to what is now the laundry room (seen right) may have been the original entryway, so there are now two adjoining hallways. Whatever it was, it is now a well-appreciated and celebrated thoroughfare. Hand-painted flowers by my artist friend Ben Peck-Whiston, along with a multicolored floral chandelier and a delicate flowery painted mirror, are the touches of beauty that the space deserves.

A strip of hooks hangs in both hallways, where jackets and coats share space with the occasional prom dress, ready and waiting for an impromptu snap when the light creates a magical moment. A cluster of wellies—some mine, some left behind by guests to lock in their opportunity to return—sit comfortably next to my basket of flowery vintage hats, also on standby for their moment to shine.

When on the way in or out, or to one of the rooms in between, my guests and I often linger in this modest but rich space to contemplate the wow of it.

RIGHT *I love how so much beauty collides at the crossroads of the laundry room, the living room, the staircase and the hallway. I'm reminded of a little chapel by way of the archway and door with its painted strap hinges. Shades of blues and teals are the common thread of the palette here, picked up in Ben Peck-Whiston's floating flowers, the crystals on the chandeliers, the rug and the mirror. Matchy-matchy is never my goal, but harmony of shades always creates a sense of calm.*

LEFT *The mismatch of a shearling coat and a tulle prom dress is somehow a perfect marriage.* **ABOVE** *A quiet moment: tokens of love and faith and a piece of art by my daughter Lily Ashwell.* **OVERLEAF** *Eye candy: stacks of faded floral fabric, both vintage and from my collections (left). Ben Peck-Whiston has applied a layer of chalky paint over his newly painted flowers to create the illusion they have been discovered beneath layers of paint (right). Door curtains keep the drafts out during winter and drawing them in the evening closes the day beautifully (page 38). My overflow basket of vintage hats adds beauty to my work or a quiet wow when I need to dress up for a festive occasion (page 39).*

PEARL

DESIGN ROOM
THE TEMPLE FOR MY CREATIVITY

This is my organized beautiful mess—my melting pot where all my projects and my designs coexist. My fabric designs are a common thread woven into multiple projects, from bedding to rugs, wallpaper, tablecloths and beyond. At first glance the space might seem like disorganized eye candy, but I know the whereabouts of every single piece of ribbon, sketch and folded piece of fabric, whether stored in a cupboard, pinned on a board or layered on the shelves. I need to be able to pivot from one project to another and have at my fingertips any element necessary to create a new tapestry.

I have been designing for 36 years now, so many of my archives are stored in this room. It is an exercise in nostalgia as well as providing inspiration for evolving and reinventing. Some elements of loveliness here are the treasures I have gathered over the years and which layer into the storytelling of my designs, the punctuation marks that create an immersion into my world.

Although one of my thoughts when I set up home in the English countryside was to slow down, that has not been my flow. Juggling deadlines and commitments in both the UK and US requires discipline on my behalf or I could be on call and working 24/7 in two different time zones. So I am mindful of the need for this space to be inspiring and peaceful.

I haven't quite fine-tuned my ability to manage my time yet, but I am very conscious of my North Star, which is to create a fully balanced life. To embrace the world of design and make-believe, but also to have time to satisfy other interests and curiosities, as well as take care of myself.

My anchors to recenter and calm my mind are to step aside and walk around my garden or to sit at the mindfully placed piano. While I can read music, I don't play well, but just tinkering and focusing on the notes sweeps my brain clear of thoughts, presenting another focus, so I can then return to my work or simply walk away completely until the next time.

RIGHT *George spends many hours on this chair, mostly happily, until my work keeps my attention for a little too long.*

OVERLEAF *My playroom. Layers of past and current work and memorabilia are all strategically placed for my process of design. The view from this room is of the walled garden and I gaze out, deep in thought, for hours. My old green harvest table is a mix of pretty projects and admin. I'm more comfortable with paper invoices and receipts, so having them on hand keeps me in order. This in turn supports my creative flow. A pair of tissue tutus made by Grace Barzyz give me daily joy.*

ABOVE *These are faux flowers in disguise and an exquisite floral burst in my office, often pulling stems for photo shoots.*

RIGHT *Angie Denny is an artisan craft maker, and her tulle miniature prom dresses are beloved by me and my customers alike. My mum played the piano beautifully, and while I can do little more than tinker. I've always owned a piano. This one isn't the most beautiful, but she plays a pretty tune and continues a legacy that's important to me.*

OVERLEAF *I have bags of ribbons and lace, some passed down from my mum and others amassed by me over the years. I keep my favorites pinned up for easy access (left).*

LOVE
Hallet Davis & Co

LEFT *The challenge of having my US light fixtures rewired, mostly without success, led me to find other solutions and these have turned into newfound loves. This lampshade is one example.*

ABOVE *My raspberry Murano glass lamp is a treasure. I'm sure the original shade had no sign of flowers or tassels, but I love the combination.*

OVERLEAF *A common sight on my design table are ingredients that together tell a bigger story. It is in the details of the details that I find tiny threads to weave into a new tapestry. Having worked for many years gathering historical elements and building up an archive of work, I have a massive library of treasures—never truly forgotten, however minuscule.*

RACHEL
SHABB
Rachel Ashwell
Couture
Making placket, gathering and sewing on Bands.

ABOVE *When I'm in my creative zone, I am smiling both inside and out. Being a business owner makes it hard to protect that smile, and sometimes it's not possible, but the passion remains in the heart, protected and safe.*
RIGHT *There's nothing quite like vintage glitter. It shines with a soft, subtle glow that I love.*

OVERLEAF *Nearly every book I've created features one of my mood boards. They are active reflections of what is current in my life, so I edit and curate frequently. Adding and letting go is a refreshing act that I am mindful about. It's a rare day I throw away something that has once been part of my story, as one day it may well return.*

Ashwell
800.550.0005

I LOVE YOU
Mummy!
GOOD LUCK
CHANEL
Be not weary in well doing

THE KITCHEN
FEASTING AND CONVERSATION

I've lived in many homes over the years, and I've mostly worked with the footprint of their existing kitchens. I've had a galley kitchen, sometimes a nook, sometimes a bit of a hodgepodge. But I've never had as large a kitchen as at Meadow Manor. The prior owners were proper bakers and cooks, unlike me. I do make a few dishes, but I wondered how my minimal needs would fill the space. I worked with what was there, repainted the cabinets, replaced a slab of marble on the vast island and updated the countertops with salvaged scaffolding boards.

Having an Aga range cooker in an English country home is somewhat signature. They are like the Rolls-Royce of stoves. There is a whole slow-living Aga lifestyle—they can take five days to heat up if turned off—and I love the romance of it all. However, life has evolved since Agas were introduced in the 1920s, and today there are options to modernize them. I had mine re-enameled with the wow of white, and the fuel source converted from oil to electricity. In the Aga world the kettle is always on the hotplate ready for tea, and Aga-made toast is a priceless experience. I hope one day to incorporate more of the slow-down of Aga living—it's a beautiful philosophy.

I was happy there was room here for a good-sized dining table and chairs, leftovers from The Prairie and Malibu, along with a spot for an oversized velvet-upholstered chair from my collection at Next. Much time is spent here having meetings around the table with the kettle on and the radio playing classical music on the BBC. I did ship over a treasured chandelier for my ultimate dining space, but as of now I haven't had success in transitioning it to meet UK wiring regulations. Instead, the area is lit by small vintage lamps and candlelight.

My collection of vintage china—a hodgepodge of colors and patterns—is piled up in multiple places, ready and at hand for everyday use. The flagstone floor is unforgiving when pieces slip out of my hands, so I am careful but not neurotic if accidents happen. I draw the line at cracks and chips for eating and drinking, but when they occur, the pieces get moved on to become vases or other decorative accents around the house. There is still a healthy supply of replacement vintage plates and cups at local flea markets and vintage shops.

I have an indulgent supply of printed and white ruffled napkins and tablecloths from my various collections. I love the quality of vintage linen as well as the exquisite handwork of the crochet and lace. I rarely use a paper napkin, as I try to celebrate what and when I eat, whether it's a quick snack alone or a feast for many.

RIGHT *The kitchen-dining room was where I first entered Meadow Manor. The original flagstone floors were an immediate heart-stopper for me, as well as the double aspect windows that create an ethereal cross light. I've had to grow into the scale of this room, as previously I've always had small kitchens. As I worked with this space, it took on many functions and became an "everything" room. The kitchen has evolved into the heart of the home, with an eclectic mix of decor from art to comfy seats and a dining table that is as happy being dressed for eating as it is for creative projects and conversations. Every square inch has found its beautiful purpose.*

LEFT *My dog George has many chairs that he has adopted around the house. He always welcomes a snuggle in this velvet chair from my collection at Next.*
ABOVE *While purple is not my favorite color, these treasures I adore.*
OVERLEAF *A vintage Bristol glass vase, art by my daughter, a watercolor held in its frame with Sellotape and a reproduction jug share space on the mantel (left). Music is an important element of my home. I have a Sonos system and typically start my day with my playlists of mantra music, transitioning to country and ending with classical or light opera. At times, I like to tune in to my iconic Roberts radio, connecting me gently to reality (right).*

House
Five

Roberts

ABOVE *I have a vast collection of antique linens collected over the years as well as a staple stream of birthday gifts from my mum. I use them every day.* **RIGHT** *My collection of vintage china is a hodgepodge of colors, patterns and quality.* **OVERLEAF** *The dining area's humble hanging candelabra was intended to be temporary, but I've grown to love it. The process of lighting the candles and snuffing out the flames to close the evening will likely not be replaced by the grandeur of my original plan. The crackled white dining table came from The Prairie, and the French chairs are from various chapters of my life, delicate yet sturdy and given extra protection by their ruffled linen seat covers.*

Greek Style

Rachel

LEFT *I love homemade cakes, but when time is short I buy a plain one and frost it imperfectly with buttercream, sprinkle it with powdered sugar, add some vintage tat and wrap the base in crepe paper. It's nearly too lovely to slice.*
ABOVE *My love of hodgepodge continues: a cut crystal glass sits with no judgment next to a jam jar, a royal memorabilia tumbler alongside fine porcelain. Beauty knows no borders.*
OVERLEAF *I love the romance of the Aga lifestyle; the backsplash behind is from Starel Stones (left). While I can't lay claim to be a full-on chef, my roast dinners are quite yummy. Billowing lace curtains and old stone are a beautiful juxtaposition (right).*

AGA

THE LITTLE LAUNDRY ROOM
THE GREATEST ROOM OF ALL

I've had many love affairs with laundry rooms. There is just something about giving a new lease of life to whatever pieces pass though. This little room handles a magnitude of laundry. Whether I've had a single guest or a houseful, I always ask them to drop their linens and towels in the laundry room corner.

I have a constant flow of photo shoots at my house, and the featured linens also go through my laundering process so that when photographed they look lived-in and not too polished. I am fairly territorial about the way these lovelies are handled, so I mostly do it all myself. There are some days when linens cascade into the hallway, which could be overwhelming for some but to me is a beautiful sight. I have reframed the chore into an act of appreciation and meditation. I do not rush the process; it is a practice. Some linens need to be soaked first, others take their own sweet time to dry.

I rarely put bed linens in the dryer. For the most part they spend time on the wood-and-pulley drying rack, or, on a guaranteed rain-free English summer's day, they hang from the garden washing line. I take time to prep them, taking them from the wash, shaking them out and manipulating the ruffles between my fingers. The end result is lovely fresh linens that may be a little rumpled but are not wrinkled and rarely need an iron.

This little engine room deserves its loving decor. The walls are painted in a barely there diluted pink and I've been collecting vintage tiles to eventually cover the whole of the back wall, but as it goes it's already lovely. My friend the artist Jorunn Mulen painted a whimsical Pierrot mural tucked away on the inward facing wall. She can be missed, but when spotted she provides an "Ahh" moment.

I purchased curtain rods from a ship's cabin supplier, and hung some leftover Prairie curtains over the washer and dryer. Little details like the tiny pink mirrored medicine cabinet contribute to making a jewel box of this much-loved space.

RIGHT *I could write a novel on my love and appreciation of laundry. While piles of laundry overflowing into the hallway might seem overwhelming, they are a common sight in my home. I see linens as loved and enjoyed, in part for how I take care of them and the joy the process brings me, which is captured in the experience for myself and my guests when they get into the beds. While I rarely use my dryer for linens, my drying rack and washing line are in constant rotation.*

OVERLEAF *This array of laces and ruffles is a sight to behold (left). Even though the laundry is a tiny room, I spend much time here, so small decorative touches like the Jorunn Mulen wall painting are worthwhile (right). Natural drying leaves lovely rumples but no wrinkles with rarely a need for ironing (page 74). I am collecting vintage tiles and over time I plan to cover the entire back wall (page 75).*

THE MIDDLE FLOOR

ROOMS TO DREAM

The floor above the busy heartbeat of the home is a space of calm and serenity. I'm learning the rhythm of hosting in the English countryside, from new friends popping by for a cup of tea to friends and family visiting from London or faraway places. Some stay overnight, others for weeks. I value the experience of sharing my world and consider all the special and welcoming details, from the teapot, cup and napkin to bed dressings and flowers. I want my guests to feel appreciated and cared for in their own little sanctuary, a welcoming room that is not over-personalized with my bits and bobs but somewhere they can linger and dream.

A GUEST ROOM
DELICATE DETAILS

This room is of lovely square proportions and overlooks the walled garden. I painted the original floorboards white, figuring there would be less chance of muddy footprints in here, but just in case, they are easily moppable.

The touch of color on the two-tone walls comes from a pale-pink paint, diluted to 50% and reaching to chair-rail height, where it meets an ice-creamy tone that covers the top half of the walls up to the ceiling. Sweet and romantic, but offset by the black fireplace, which I opted to leave unchanged rather than painting it white, and where I often place flowers for shoots or guests.

The room is a symphony of beautiful pieces that have played starring roles in their previous lives, which you may recognize from my past books. The rug was relocated from the Meadow Manor—my new home was named in its honor—at The Prairie. The floral carved vanity with its flaking green paintwork is from Lilliput Lodge at The Prairie, while the creamy blue-trimmed armoire is from my Malibu cottage many years ago. As I'm always looking to create calm for sleep, there are only a couple of gentle paintings and a faint, barely there ballerina by Jorunn Mulen painted on the wall over the radiator.

I was thrilled to find a set of three frilly silk lampshades at my local flea market. They were intended as a temporary solution until I could have my twinkling chandeliers installed, but I have grown to love them and they have found their permanent home here.

LEFT *This traditional chair with a white slipcover, made from an old French linen sheet by my friend Rebecca, is in my eyes timeless and simply lovely. A scrap of Bennison's Roses fabric commands attention, even though only used for the seat cushion.*

ABOVE *Imperfection in its finest form. Mixing fabrics in upholstery is a good economical option and ideal for an eclectic aesthetic. The white slipcover is generously tailored, with a barely gathered ruffle.* **RIGHT** *The perfect bluey-pink silky gown is part of my traveling girl's collection of mostly tulle prom dresses. The delicacy of this dress adds another vibe.*

OVERLEAF *My Shabby Chic Floral Ikat collection was tricky to develop—getting the fading to the point of barely there is a process that takes time (left). Vintage lamps are such treasures, with details and painted finishes that are rarely found today (right). I always have vintage lighting rewired to be safe, and the twisted cloth cord adds a pretty detail.*

shabby girl

E
THE DARK SIDE
FALL FASHION

ABOVE *So much about this lamp is a misfit: it is too small for the space and the shade doesn't fit, but somehow the misfit fits.*

RIGHT *Hydrangea curtains from my Next collection: puddling and gathered just enough. The hanging silk lampshade was never meant to stay forever, but likely will–the pale pink under-ruffle is a divine touch. The bed is another treasure that crossed the Atlantic in a container. Confusion arose due to the UK/US size classifications, but I fixed the problem with the help of a carpenter. Today it is fit for a king or queen.*

OVERLEAF *This guest room is a memory lane of experiences. Each piece evokes the history we have shared, now in place for new memories to be made.*

LEFT *There are several non-working fireplaces on this middle floor. Heat isn't really needed thanks to the handsome reproduction radiators I installed, so I often celebrate the fireplaces decoratively. In this case, a romantic blousy bouquet by Toria Britten contrasts with its dark surroundings.*

ABOVE *My friend Jorunn Mulen left behind a whimsical gift on one of her visits: a beautiful ballerina deep in thought, painted on the two-tone pink wall. She is a calming presence that in no way intrudes on the peace and quiet of this guest room, but to me she is breathtaking.*

THE BATHROOM FOR GUESTS
PEACEFUL PAMPERING

When I took ownership of the home, this bathroom was a little tired, as it had never been updated since the prior owners had small children. All of my decor and design choices were focused on refreshing the space while remaining sympathetic to the legacy and age of the house. For this bathroom, I elected for traditional reproduction faucets/taps. While it is always tempting to buy original vintage hardware, plumbing is tricky enough without navigating the inevitable restoration.

I spent hours researching tile options, wanting to include details from days gone by while maintaining a tranquil aesthetic. I was happy to find a touch of tradition in the decorative trim, while artisan tiles in the palest green combined with fresh white created the balance I wanted to achieve. Little touches of whimsy by way of a hanging vintage mirror and a floral painted miniature table soften the sea of tiles. The lace panel curtain I hand-sewed myself; it's a little wonky but charming and contributes a moment of soft imperfection. As always with guest bathrooms, I add special toiletries, fluffy towels and robes, always striving to create a luxury hotel experience.

Leading to the bathroom is a landing with a mix of original and reclaimed pine boards. There were some random dark patches on the planks that I didn't much care for, but after my failure to refinish the floors in the living room, I decided to celebrate these and asked my artist friend Ben Peck-Whiston to freehand some florals on them (as seen opposite page 240). And so, a detail I wanted to discard became a showstopper.

I am mindful of the emotional and aesthetic flow when making decorating choices. I always consider the transitions from hallways into the rooms to which they lead. In this instance, the soft blue-green tiles of the bathroom flow smoothly into the hallway and stairs. The teal-painted stair runner is a smokier, richer shade than the tiles but of the same palette. Painting the runner in an eggshell finish and leaving the edges white is a lovely way to add color and interest to a well-trodden staircase.

RIGHT *Bathroom renovations are the most daunting, with so many details to consider, large and small. This was another space where I considered a dusty, smoky palette, but in the end kept within my comfort zone of soothing pale blue-green artisan tiles.*

OVERLEAF *I tried to steer myself away from anything too fussy and feminine in here, but I couldn't resist the temptation of the rose swag vanity mirror (left). It's a little rough around the edges, which I think keeps it from being too sweet. As small as it is, it's very functional, with a built-in shelf and drawer. Polished nickel is my favorite finish for bathroom fixtures, as it will age with grace. I am always collecting or being gifted extra-special toiletries, which I save for my guests to enjoy during their stay (right).*

Burlington

BRIDIE HALL
DIANA
A Divine Power
INTAGLIO SOAP
Made by hand in London
SHABBY CHIC

ABOVE *I hand-sewed these cotton lace panels, hence the wonky side seam. I'm not great at sewing, but it was too hard to find someone to do such a tiddly job, so I simply did it myself.*

RIGHT *The pastel tiles are from Bert & May and the white artisan tiles and ornate border are both from Fired Earth. My dear friend the artist Laurence Amélie gifted me this teeny abstract painting of peonies. The vintage floral lidded ceramic pot below is the perfect counterpoint.*

THE LEFTOVER ROOM
THE BEAUTY OF IMPERMANENCE

Initially, this room was to be a second guest bathroom, and I even went so far as installing all the plumbing. But, partly because of the expense, and the realization that another bathroom wasn't really necessary, it has eventually become the all-important "leftover" room.

The walls were set to be papered with a design from my wallpaper collection, but at a certain point I decided to let some of the raw plaster walls have their moment. It gives me the versatility of different backdrops when I do photo shoots in this room, as well as paying homage to my love of incompleteness.

I was ready to reupholster the French chair, as I had done for the rest of the suite I had purchased, but I decided on a whim to leave the back of the chair open, beautifully framing a portion of the back wall. I find many incomplete or unfinished treasures on my flea-market hunts, often wondering why they were left undone.

The French daybed often plays out the story of "The Princess and the Pea," as it sets the stage for many of my projects. It is somewhere I can combine all my frills, ruffles and palettes, and even though all my ranges of bed dressings are beautiful on their own, I can see the common threads of my designs playing off each other when they are layered together, mixing and matching.

This is my visual storytelling space. Flowers, lace and tutus come and go, leaving an assortment of ballet slippers and ribbons housed in the non-working fireplace. They are no longer used for their original purpose, but still as beautiful as they ever were.

There have been times when all the bedrooms in the house are full and the leftover room serves as an extra sleeping space. Its occupant gets to slip into the decoration of the most recent storytelling, and dreamy dreams are had.

LEFT *This room is never forgotten, but I've not yet decided on a permanent use and maybe never will. It is in constant transition with my samples and collections. As I pass by, I can decide if I love what I see or if maybe a design tweak is needed, so in a way, this room is like an artist's canvas.*

OVERLEAF *There is so much beauty in the incompleteness of this chair: exposed canvas padding and stitches, evidence of nail marks, intricate carving and a shabby paint finish (left). All of this would be missed if it were restored. It is juxtaposed pleasingly with a pearly silver tufted ottoman, a nod to tradition with a rock-and-roll twist (right). From my wallpaper collection, Chinoiserie Pink and Gold gives a touch of delicacy but remains somewhat neutral. Painted plywood flooring sets the stage for layers of rugs. Some are vintage and one is the floral Pink Bouquet from my collection at Next.*

LEFT *Ruffles, lace and rumpled bed dressings from my Shabby Chic collection, displaying the full spectrum of my preferred palette, come together like a virtual painting.*

ABOVE *Ballet slippers with trailing ribbons decorate the empty fireplace as part of today's storytelling.*

THE GRAND WHITE BEDROOM
DREAMY LUXURY

A beautiful wow of a grand white room, this space has perfect proportions and magnificent light. Sometimes I dress it minimally in white, with the vintage furniture offering gentle shades of color. But it can also handle a glorious ensemble of florals and flowers. It offers a world of gloriously comfortable reality within a frame of make-believe. The beautiful cast of characters decorating this luxurious room, from the curtains to the pink velvet loveseat, the slipcovered headboard and the sumptuous bedding is the romantic world of Shabby Chic at its finest.

I was happy to find original wooden floorboards under the existing carpet and, as with the other bedrooms on this level, I painted them white. They have some dings and gaps, but that is all part of the shabby world. I spent a meaningful part of my budget on replacing all the radiators throughout the house with high-functioning reproduction cast-iron versions. To me they are a handsome design element to be proudly seen and their warmth much appreciated.

I tried a few soft pastel shades of paint in this room, but once again came back to white. But I did my signature treatment by installing a chair rail throughout and added Anaglypta paper below, which I painted with a slightly glossier finish. This adds some texture and detail to break up the vastness of the painted walls.

Along with the petite slipcovered chair, this room was easily able to accommodate a mushy loveseat sofa—such an indulgence. The pink velvet slipcover and mix-and-match Rose Majesty covers give a touch of both luxury and charm, inviting and so, so comfy. The curtains are overdyed Royal Bouquet, one of my signature prints. They hung for many years in my daughter's room during her flowery era. All the furniture, the accessories, the vases, side tables—everything had a previous life either in Texas or in Malibu. The only recent acquisition is the lovely full-length mirror leaning against the wall, which I unearthed in a local antiques market.

As large as this room is, it lacks storage, so my traveling vintage prom dresses come and go as guests need space on the wardrobe rail. In the meantime, they offer decor in all their girly glory. The grand proportions of this room easily absorb multiple abundant floral displays worthy of a five-star hotel, designed asymmetrically of course: imperfectly perfect.

LEFT *Flowers on flowers are the backdrop for another charming vintage lamp. It is made of ombre raspberry glass with a mismatched pleated, fringed and trim-embellished shade; so many details for something so small.*

OVERLEAF *The stripped wood floor of the hallway transitions to the white-painted planks of the bedroom, partially covered by a somewhat tattered vintage rug (left). A duck-egg blue vanity with slightly folky engraving is an echo of the hallway's dainty table in the same hue. Floral hats, selected for their palette, are placed for some prettiness until required for dress-up. The hand-carved painted lamp commands attention with its tasseled shade, layering into the multiple floral subjects of this room (right). This is the most favored guest room—the proportions are grand and the light is breathtaking (pages 104–105). I dress this room according to my guests' preferences, whether simple and white or dressed in a glorious symphony of mix-and-match bed linens.*

FLORAL BED DRESSINGS

I have been designing floral bedding for several decades. I love large, colorful floral bouquets as much as faded, ditsy flowers. My philosophy has always been to mix and match and layer from collection to collection.

Many of my prints are inspired by vintage floral scraps. Sometimes I rework a print from my archives: scaling up a petite bloom into a larger flower, perhaps adding a bird or butterfly and, of course, changing the colors. The process of getting the palette just right is a long one. The initial phase is called "reviewing a strike off," which is where I see a small test of the print on some fabric to observe how the colors fall. Usually some tweaking is needed, as I am non-negotiable when it comes to color. Pink is often a star in my ensemble of colors, and it's the trickiest of them all. My signature pink favors a bluey tone rather than a salmon, coral or yellow note, and fortunately I have the patience of a saint when it comes to getting it right.

Even though there is quite a diversity across my prints, they all share a common thread in the library of colors I consistently pull from, as well as in the delicacy of the artwork—these are the tenets that let them layer and belong together. Quite often I pull out a duvet or pillowcase from my library and it's like seeing an old friend. Like a song, memories are associated with the era when that design was a constant, but they are truly timeless; there is always time to revisit these cherished patterns and layer them back into the old and the new.

RIGHT *I have kept almost every print I have ever designed over the course of the past three decades. Somehow, whatever era they come from, they all layer together well. If a print needs a refresh, I overdye it with a different color in my laundry sink—often it will then provide new inspiration for my work.*

OVERLEAF *The light can play tricks on paint colors. After a few attempts at various shades of pastels, I reverted to bright white with a glossier finish on the wallpapered lower section. The nice thing about paint is that it is easy to redo later if I decide to try some color, maybe starting below the chair rail. It is such an indulgence to have space for this Shabby Chic pale-pink squishy loveseat in a bedroom. Continuing the burst of flowers from every corner of the room, the cascading asymmetrical florals designed by Toria Britten are timeless and luxurious (page 110). The little slipper chair moves from room to room and has an assortment of charming baggy slipcovers—it has great versatility, a chameleon of sorts (page 111).*

MY SUITE
A PLACE TO DREAM

Serenity and tranquillity are my mantras for every decision I make in regard to my bedroom. It's a large room, so it needed a bed of equal scale. Another lesson I had to learn was that an American queen is the equivalent of an English king, causing quite some confusion when it came to my mattresses and bed dressings. The white-painted bed, which had been squeezed into my rented country cottage, filling the room from wall to wall, is now able to breathe. I typically prefer white poplin ruffled bedding for myself. So many of my days are spent with a focus on florals that for a few hours each day I need to rest and reset my creative brain, even if it's while I am sleeping.

I have always been drawn to a white bedroom. However, I did add a couple of embellishments here by way of a tonal creamy border at the top of the walls and a soft rubbed-back stencil over the non-working fireplace. All sit well with the white-painted wooden floors.

I found having to commit to the placement of the wall lights challenging, because it was before I knew exactly what would go where, so I elected to place sconces only over the fireplace and mismatched table lamps flanking the bed. The chandelier leans towards the world of shabby more than chic, as the crystals need restringing and the shades are threadbare, but I have accepted that it may well be a project that I never quite get round to.

My favorite curtains in the whole house are these, which I had made locally. I visited a fabric remnant warehouse looking for a powdery pink silk, but instead found a lovely dusty blue, which I love so much. The curtain maker was talented at her craft, and the finished drapes were perfect, but they have been made a little less so by me letting out the ruched header for a little irregularity—because the imperfection has to be perfect.

I usually lean mirrors against the wall rather than hanging them. I enjoy the philosophy of impermanence and detachment, and there is a casualness I enjoy in something that can otherwise be formal. The matching chair to the one in the leftover room (see pages 94–99) received a full reupholster and has been personalized with an embroidered R, perfect for me. The Shabby Chic white linen slipcovered chair is another chair largely enjoyed by George. While the chair itself is over 20 years old, over time I have replaced the feather down-wrapped cushions and made new slipcovers. Like all of my Shabby Chic furniture that I've lived with and loved for upwards of 20 years, it holds precious memories, but is easily refreshed, keeping shabbiness at bay.

RIGHT *My heavenly hallway. By day, the light streams through the window, highlighting my half-painted tonal wall. At the close of the day, there is a soothing ritual in knowing that the hallway leads into my place to dream.*

OVERLEAF *All of my bedrooms over the years have had a common thread, whether grand or petite, by the water or in the countryside. I have always strived for simplicity, the purest form of beauty. There is a sense of luxury with lofty fresh white cotton Shabby Chic linens, a timeworn but still elegant chandelier and silk taffeta window dressings, with heavy lining, emulating a ball gown, and little else.*

LEFT *Shabby Chic stays true throughout my home. With a nod to both, this chair captures it all.* **ABOVE** *A candid shot of me, taking a moment.* **OVERLEAF** *Ruching and ruffles are abundant and gorgeous here—I give thanks as I draw the curtains at the end of the day (left). I am very selective as to what I place on my nightstand (right). There is no thoughtless clutter in this sanctuary, only items of enough beauty to see when I first awake and before I close my eyes to sleep. Doves symbolize peace, love, healing and grace, beautiful energy for my sleeping space (page 120). I like mirrors in my bedroom for their decorative qualities (page 121). Often the glass is cloudy and tarnished, while the frame tells a story.*

SUPPLY
ALL YOUR
NEED

JORK WEISMANN
Asleep at the Chateau
DAMIANI
VOGUE LIVING
HOME DESIGN: HOLLYWOOD, NEW YORK
MAY 7, 2012
Cate Blanchett
DECEMBER/JANUARY 2009

LEFT *This is the view as I open my eyes. Soothing and romantic. Enough beauty for my eyes while calming for my soul. Working on the various floral painted installations throughout the house with Ben Peck-Whiston is a collaborative process. Initially I wanted multiple flowers here, but in the end, one bouquet remains to complement the simpler stencil.*
ABOVE *This chandelier leans to the shabby side of chic. I added the set of three tattered petite shades, in keeping with the overall faded elegance.*

BOUDOIR BEAUTY
PRETTY PRIMPING

I adore my boudoir and dressing room, but it has crossed my mind that such a place would be deserving of someone who is more of a pamperer than I am. However, the space was already there, so I decided to embrace the indulgence.

I found this magical vanity some years back at my friend's store Lark Vintage, well before I had anywhere for it to go. It waited patiently in storage for several years before it finally found its perfect placement. It is gloriously shabby as well as very functional. It took me a while to get comfortable sitting in front of a full-length mirror, all the while thinking that, in its past life, the mirror must have reflected someone much more glamorous than me.

I continued the white-painted floors from the bedroom into the boudoir and, once again, I left the plaster raw—it has a beautiful patina. I love the way it has dried to different hues depending on the structure and material of the wall, leaving pleasingly random patches.

My little bits and bobs of beauty products are kept easily accessible so I remember to use them. And even though some fancy shoes would complete the picture, my favorite cowboy boots are always in waiting—quite the juxtaposition to the romantic surroundings.

And so while, as with some other rooms at Meadow Manor, my boudoir beauty is a larger space than I am used to, I am leaning into the notion of enjoying the luxury of this beautiful boudoir. During daylight hours, no other light is needed due to the ethereal sunshine that streams through my lace panels. This space, I am learning, encourages me to slow down and take a little more time to focus on myself.

RIGHT *I love the textures of this room: the raw plaster walls and the painted floors. The star of the show is the exquisite finish and scale of the vanity, which contains makeup and toiletries. Because of the time-worn element to the elegance, I'm not intimidated by the space, but I have yet to grow into it. Truth is, I'm not much of pamperer, more of a powder my nose and run. But I'm leaning into believing there is a reason I inherited this space.*

MY BATHROOM
BATHING GLAMOUR

My boudoir leads into my glamorous, scrumptious bathroom. I have moved around from house to house over the years, from Malibu to Los Angeles to my little rented country cottage. However big or small my homes have been, I've always had little bathrooms. Sometimes they had a shower and tub combined, and sometimes the two were separate, but either way my daily bathing was my sacred time.

Over the years, I've taken notes of elements I have enjoyed from beautiful hotel stays, loving the luxury, the glamour and the practicality. So, when the time came to design and decorate my bathing space, I was well prepared. I started with a blank slate within the footprint of the original bathroom and plotted out what would go where.

I researched tile companies, wanting to embrace the 400-year-old house with some traditional details while also imagining a fresh and peaceful aesthetic. I found a lacy textured square tile—the ornate Highgrove tile and border from Original Style—and what I thought was a whisper-pink tile, finished with a porcelain rim. I thought this pairing would satisfy my vision, but the whisper-pink tile turned out to be Barbie pink when installed. Barbie had to go, so she was chipped away and replaced with a more peaceful gray-white marble.

An original pair of wooden shutters surrounds a picture-perfect window over the tub, giving a moment of cottage among the glamour. A heated towel rail, a two-legged pedestal sink, which I also have in my California home, and a most beautiful free-standing tub checked the boxes of my luxury hotel-inspired bathroom. I accessorized with some perfectly distressed vintage mirrors to bring some shabby into all the chicness.

No doubt this is a dream bathroom. It has been featured in many magazines and would get a five-star rating. Slowly I am falling in love with her. But this process has taught me that my comfort lies in humble fancy, and even though this glamorous bathroom has everything I visualized, I realize I got caught up in a dream that didn't align with my heart. That can happen in life—making dreams our reality is possible, we just have to make sure the dream fits into our truth and heart.

LEFT *While high heels and fashionable shoes would complement this boudoir beautifully, my beaten-up beloved cowboy boots are typically on standby, ready for nearly every day and most every occasion.*

LEFT AND ABOVE *I've come a long way since my first bedsit with a communal bathroom servicing multiple flats, where coins were needed to fill the meter for a hottish shower. Now here I have beautiful eye candy: a grand bathtub and a tiny table, a Venetian mirror and a hodgepodge of vintage bottles and fading roses.*

OVERLEAF *Each day I fall a little more in love with this room. It is taking time, but not because it is not completely lovable. Until now, I have played the role of a princess, and the queen inside is yet to be revealed. The marble tiles, bathtub and statuesque pedestal sink are all from Fired Earth. I also love the wooden shutters, lacy tiles and nickel faucets/taps.*

THE TOP FLOOR

HEAVENLY ROOMS

I was introduced as a young girl to attic living. Sometimes they were makeshift spaces, up a rickety ladder and through a trap door with little to no light—in this case my dad's man cave of sorts—ducking between beams and navigating wobbly plywood floors, while others had been converted into an actual living space. Either way, I learned early on the value of attics and, for me, their heavenly qualities.

THE PRINCESS-PINK ROOM
THE JEWEL BOX

When I was a young teenager, I had an attic bedroom. It was my first proper bedroom of a reasonable size where I have memories of sitting on the floor listening to my LPs—my own private space. This was before I paid much attention to aesthetics, but if I had, my room would have looked just like this princess-pink bedroom. Although it is quite small, it is not pokey—and being at the top of the house means it bathes in heavenly light.

The walls are an example of the beauty of incompleteness. Initially they were pinker than I planned, partly due to the way the light dances around. Ben Peck-Whiston hand-painted some tossed floral bouquets for me, rubbed back to barely there but still adding quite the wow factor. In time I painted over the pink walls with white chalk paint and wiped much of it off with a damp cloth, creating inconsistencies, and I rather like the effect just the way it turned out.

This room is used the least as far as guests go, because of its location and petite size. But I often pop in to visit, as this is the room my younger self would have loved. There is no storage, but a wooden wardrobe rack is put in place when needed, sometimes for guests and sometimes for bedding collections with their ruffles on show, waiting for their moment to be photographed.

There is a carousel of bedding changes for photography for my multiple projects. I forget what I put there from one shoot to the next, so there's always an "Ahh!" moment when I check in to see how it was last dressed. The final twinkle touch is one of my few American chandeliers that was able to be rewired to meet UK wiring regulations, saving the best for last.

LEFT *I consider this the jewel-box bedroom, small but rich with treasures. Beautiful layers and lacy textures sit alongside vintage floral curtains, a crocheted bedspread and ruffly shams. A twinkling chandelier is silhouetted against the softest pink walls with floral embellishments.*

OVERLEAF *A delicate raspberry watercolor of a dancer by Jorunn Mulen is casually taped to the wall, offset by the rough, textural surface behind it (left). Fuchsia florals cascade down a forever-to-keep mint green and cream nightstand (right).*

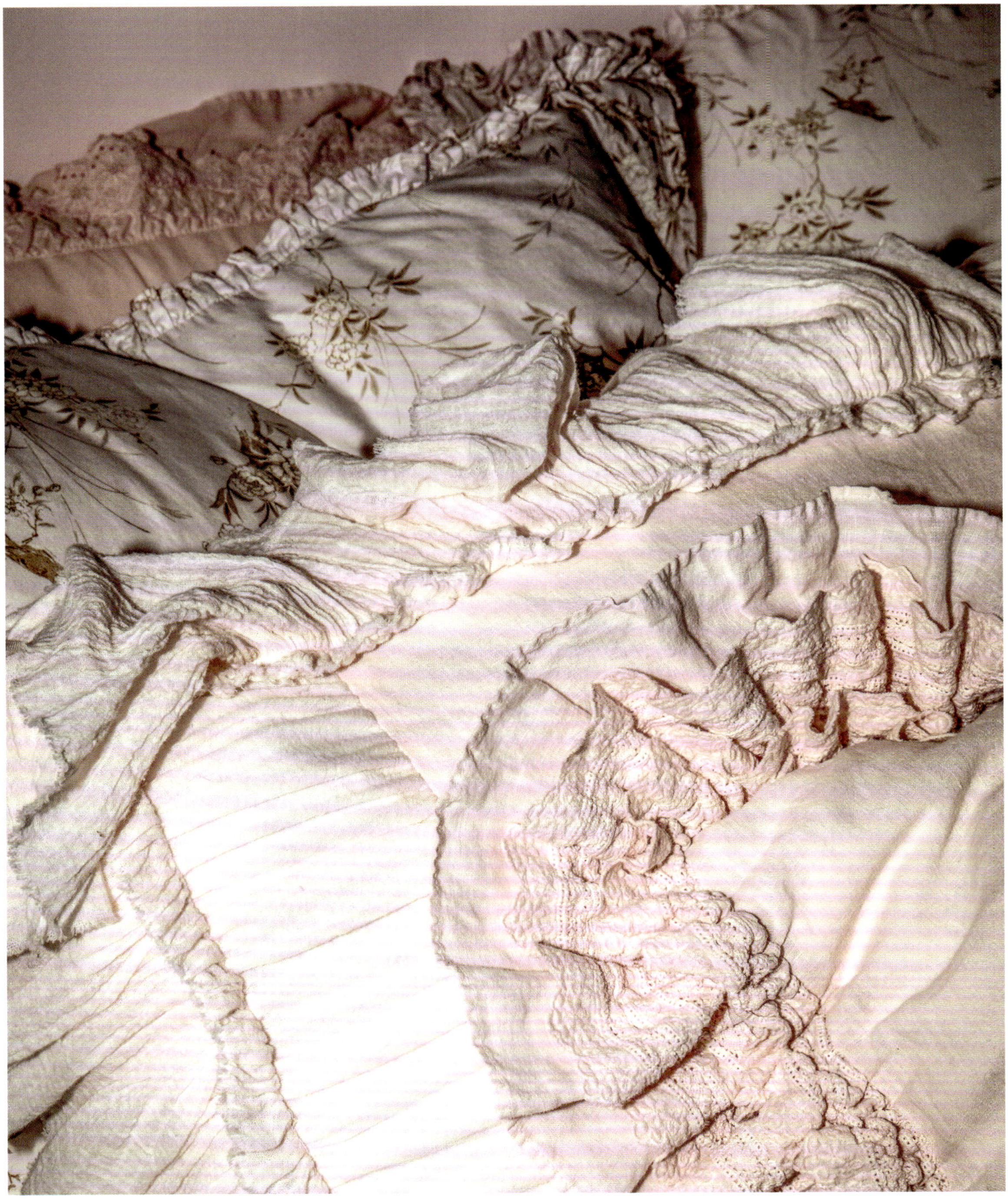

LEFT *Many photo shoots take place in this cosy guest room with its low ceilings and rustic beams. The wooden wardrobe rack is used by guests as well as linens poised for their next portrait.*
ABOVE *Frills of all sorts—cotton, linen and gauze. Some are vintage, some are my archival designs, others are samples of yet-to-be launched designs.*

OVERLEAF *Evidence of rumples without wrinkles thanks to my hand-touched process, manipulating the ruffles as they dry. Little details make all the difference (left). One of a pair of cherished pale-pink glass lamps with drops—I love them so. It took time and patience to get them working and rewired with a white cloth-covered cord (right).*

THE BATHROOM
HUMBLE FANCY

My intention for this top-floor bathroom was to refrain from my tendency to be romantic and genteel and instead to have a sense of warmth and rustic charm. Original beams set into the walls complement the white artisan tiles I installed. I chose a reproduction sink with an Edwardian but utility aesthetic and simple lever porcelain faucets/taps, juxtaposed with a delicate etched frameless mirror. All combined to create the balance of my intentions.

I gave much consideration to the decision of whether to keep the original bathtub or switch it out for a shower. Once I decided that guests would likely favor a shower, the pitched ceiling dictated the only spot that could accommodate the height needed. The grand, luxurious shower is tucked away behind the cheese board-clad, hand-stenciled wall.

Although this is a small room, I didn't compromise on any little detail and was sure to layer in luxury, humbly wherever possible. Even in a small space, I always like to place pieces of free-standing furniture in bathrooms, layered with some vintage touches. I enjoy the element of texture and softness they contribute to the sea of shiny tiles and hard surfaces. In addition, I have a few simple non-negotiables for guest bathrooms: fresh toiletries, pretty packaging and fluffy towels. An easily executed, meaningful and welcoming gesture.

My hard lessons were in negotiating the UK's strict electrical regulations for bathrooms. I learned that all lighting must be situated a certain amount of distance from water unless the bulb is fully concealed, so no pretty, twinkly chandeliers over the basin. But I was happy that my miniature floral wall sconce was considered safe over the window, a punctuation mark of romance among the otherwise minimal decor. A few yards of scrap lace afforded me to make a window dressing, which creates a lovely frame for looking over the tiled rooftops of the property. Truly charming.

LEFT *Neutral tones alongside shades of dusty sage and teal was my palette of choice for this bathroom. It is pretty and romantic with a rustic flair. I made a cushion for the folding bench for comfort as a soft touch. Adding to the rustic charm, Ben Peck-Whiston hand painted a simple stencil onto the cheese boards on the wall.*

OVERLEAF *An etched vintage mirror and porcelain shelf combine to create a vanity of sorts in this small, low-ceilinged space (left). The hardware store cut-glass light fixture satisfied the UK regulations for bathroom lights. For the lower half of the walls, I chose simple artisan square white tiles that continue the rustic aesthetic (right).*

OFFICINA
S.M.NOVELLA
FIRENZE
OLIO
COSMETICO
zangra
ARCADE

H
FIRED
C
FIRED

ABOVE *A little sage-themed story of a floral oil painting, old green labeled bottle and a charming pottery dish. I like adding pretty decorative details to soften the hard surfaces in a bathroom.*

RIGHT *This little chair slipcovered in a tropical print moves around the house. I never in my wildest dreams planned to keep the green palm leaves and yellow parrot, as neither the colors nor the design falls into my repertoire, but sometimes I surprise myself when I keep an open mind.*

THE BLUE BEDROOM
THE MAN CAVE

Most men who visit Meadow Manor gravitate to this room. Maybe that's because it's the most hidden away and hard to find, or because the one source of light, from the tiny window that overlooks the front lawn, creates a sense of near-complete privacy up here. However, I do forewarn guests that I can hear every sneeze and snore, as this room is directly above my sleeping space. With little insulation and a wide-open wood-plank floor, privacy is compromised. I installed cheeseboard flooring in this room and the princess-pink room, as the original floors up here were just plywood.

I pared back my appetite for twinkles in here, knowing my son would likely choose this room on his visits. I don't know if one could consider the hanging light fixture masculine, as it is a bit like a crocheted hat. To some, perhaps, it will go unnoticed, but I think it's divine. I am on a constant search for pretty little table lamps. For this room I recently purchased a pair with metal bases and porcelain shades, with details such as cloth-covered cord that are rarely found in today's manufacturing.

I kept the tones of the furnishings here to shades of blue including the lower half of the walls themselves. The paint color is curiously called Cabbage White by Farrow & Ball but is a true, albeit very pale, blue. There is only a teal-blue vintage cabinet for storage, but guests do have access to a wardrobe rack through the adjoining door, which leads to the room of treasures.

RIGHT *Even though this room has been referred to as a man cave, the turquoise voile embroidered bedcover and overdyed blue Victorian sham is a soothing sight, especially in summer months when the room at the top can get quite warm.*

LEFT *I always loved the colors and patina of the furniture I would find on my flea-market shopping escapades in Texas. This teal blue cabinet journeyed across the ocean to join me at Meadow Manor. I was drawn to the painting for its colors, but on a closer look realized it is quite lovely. The flowers tie in with the colors and the rustic charm of this attic room.*
ABOVE *The crocheted lampshade was a long-ago felicitous flea-market find and is the perfect shape, color and size for this quirky little room.*

THE LINEN ROOM
A ROOM OF TREASURES

Once my laundry has been through its meditative process on the ground floor, its resting place is in the top-floor linen room. This space had not been finished when I took ownership of the house, so there was a moment to consider what its use would be. I briefly thought of adding an extra bathroom, but for now, at least, I want to experience a proper linen room that feels like the stock room in one of my former stores.

I opted to keep the pinky palette of the raw plaster walls, but sealed with a matt clear varnish finish. This is a commonly found technique in older English homes and it creates a lovely patina. Having a tiny window in here was a plus, as with only a minimal source of light peeping through, the fabrics are not in danger from fading on the fold lines.

Along with my personal archives of Shabby Chic bedding and soft furnishings, I also hold samples from multiple license programs here and need to keep every item in good order. Shelves are wrapped in a patchwork of wallpaper from my collection, with little brass sleeve labels to identify what is what. Along with the order, I love the experience and energy of this room. I fold the linens carefully to make sure ruffles and lace trims are visible, as the combination of trims, prints and palettes is a visual symphony to my eyes. There is a spiritual aspect to this space where all my years of love and passion for design come together. The treasures are rephotographed from time to time and I use this repository to draw inspiration for new designs. It is my room of treasures from my life's work, and my Virgin Mary presides quietly over it in prayer and gratitude.

I also have quite a collection of Shabby Chic white poplin bedding that is housed in a separate linen cupboard. These are the staples of my bedding ranges, every bit as valuable and loved as my room of colorful treasures.

LEFT *I'm always on the lookout for lofty eiderdowns, soft and scrumptious and in an assortment of sizes, stitching and prints. They are a lovely additional layer on a bed or sofa on a cold winter's night.*

OVERLEAF *The journey of my laundry continues. Once air- or line-dried on the ground floor, it makes its way up to the top-floor linen room. I enjoy the ritual of folding my linens, taking care to let the ruffles have plenty of room on the shelves so they don't get mushed. For me, my world of laundry is all about process and patience. Mother Mary is tucked in the corner for a soothing spiritual presence.*

STD PC

ABOVE *The cotton lace shade was originally on a table lamp, but it was transformed with an antique brass ceiling rose and a cloth-covered cord and now hangs perfectly in place.*

RIGHT *My blue trestle table is my laundry folding spot, as well as contributing a welcome pop of color against the raw plaster walls. Being an attic, the eaves are low, but there's just enough height to stand in the middle of the room. The wardrobe rack is a place for pause as I gather linens for their journey back down the stairs. It's also handy for guests staying in the adjoining bedroom, who are typically amazed when they open the little door in their room to discover the room of treasures.*

THE LONG BARN

SANCTUARY OF HEARTS

My love of guest cottages goes way back. I love the intimacy of these small independent structures. Years ago, I had a little cottage in Malibu with a tiny little guest house, then later at The Prairie, my B&B in Texas, there were multiple guest cottages, all decorated with a balance of beauty, comfort and function.

So when I purchased Meadow Manor, I was thrilled to learn that an old dairy barn had already been converted into a separate living space. All the hard work of sympathetically restoring the structure and installing the electrics and plumbing was done and ready for me to create my world: a sumptuous guest cottage where friends and family could settle in during their stay.

The barn has the best views on the property, an unobstructed protected vista, just like a picture postcard of the rambling Somerset hills. It has a real spiritual quality, similar to a church with its soaring beamed ceilings, so my choices of decor obviously had to embrace that experience as a starting point.

The Long Barn describes itself well: it's a long barn, with no hallway, so its rooms lead into one another. There is a separate kitchen, then the dining area flows into the living room and a wall divides the bedroom from the bathroom. Three mirroring barn doors separate off each symmetrical section. Windows line the walls, front and back, bringing in magnificent light during the longer days of summer. Rain and wind create their own entertainment factor, with a wood-burning stove for extra warmth and romance. I opted for linen curtains, mainly for privacy and as a soft frame for the expanse of windows.

I have given the Long Barn a modern and minimal country aesthetic, using the textures of the building materials and furnishings alike, but it is still a luxurious, carefully considered space with a soulful and spiritual aura. Plaster walls left raw are offset with epoxy-painted cement floors. Exposed beams complement the blond stone pillars that frame all the windows. The interior is made inviting by mushy and whimsical furnishings. An oversized Ladbrook slipcovered sofa from my Shabby Chic collection and raw wood furniture create the anchors of the color palette. Throws are on hand for impromptu snuggles while watching the tall grasses billow in the breeze.

RIGHT *Many a long-distance traveler has stayed in this guest barn. Multiple visits from George are guaranteed, as he stops by on his wanders through the meadow at the back. Both warm summer breezes and winter winds circle the meadow and the wide-open spaces.*

ABOVE *A vintage watercolor sketchbook is left on view to provide inspiration.*
RIGHT *When my container of furniture set sail from the US, I had not yet bought Meadow Manor. However, I knew every beautiful thing would find a home. This is the only room that could fit this majestic Shabby Chic Ladbrook sofa. The cathedral-like beams welcomed an oversized chandelier.*
OVERLEAF *The barn only has one bedroom, so extra guests sleep on the daybed and sofa (left). The modest dining area is sufficient for guests, who mostly walk over to the main house for communal eating (right).*

Simplex

OFFICINA
DI
S.M.NOVELLA
FIRENZE
FONDATA NEL 1612
ELISIR
DI ROSE

PREVIOUS PAGES *The small yet luxurious kitchen contains everything practical and is very lovely (left). A few oil paintings on board are casually propped up, with no need for permanence (right).*
ABOVE AND RIGHT *French ruffled milk glass shades are easy to come by, but getting all the bits needed to make them function as lights and then installing the antique cloth cord was an exercise in patience. However, in a room with little else to distract, they are spectacular. A bed dressed in soft white Shabby Chic linens against a raw plaster wall is the epitome of simplicity and serenity.*

RESTING TRAVELERS
UNCOMPROMISED LUXURY

While most of my guests meander over to the main house for communal snacking and feasting, the kitchen here serves as a safety net for jet-lagged travelers who are hungry at odd hours. I replaced the doors on the existing cabinets with handmade reclaimed fronts, inspired by the spa at Babington House, my local branch of Soho House. The stove/cooker is from Bertozzini and the antique brass faucets are from deVOL. The left-hand wall of the kitchen has an odd slant to it, leftover from its dairy farm life, but I have let it be—it's all part of the experience of acceptance and my love of the Japanese philosophy of *wabi-sabi*, which is about finding beauty in imperfection, impermanence and simplicity.

I installed my signature open shelving, with enough room to accommodate everyday needs along with a few vintage treasures. A free-standing vintage cabinet adds a moment of uniqueness and function. The teeniest of windows, with a magnificent view, sits above the sink. I love preparing the Long Barn for friends and family alike, taking care of every little detail, including having a fly swat and mop on hand for the inevitable pesky flies or muddy footprints.

I gave much thought to the bedroom. One wall would have accommodated more generous nightstands, but placing the bed on the opposite smaller wall, with a majestic view on waking, was the compromise. With no real space for lamps on the small nightstands, I hung ruffly porcelain shades from the ceiling, which are vintage yet have a minimal appearance. The bed is a simple wood platform, allowing for the abundance of white, fresh fluffy bedding to take center stage. With no storage I decided there was a perfect spot for a shabby moment: a large, mirror-paneled French armoire for an element of grandeur among the simplicity.

The bathroom is both petite and grand in equal measure. I chose not to do any construction, so I worked with the walls already in place, which dictated a small sink but a massive shower. I built a cabinet for the basin to sit upon, offering a little bit of storage—charming and functional enough for short stays. The shower, converted from a storeroom within the original structure, is unexpectedly large, but stunning, with white artisan tiles, polished nickel faucets/taps and fluffy white towels on a vintage rack. I have a deep yearning to have my own five-star hotel one day, so I'm learning the ropes here.

I always ask my guests for feedback after their stay, and "heaven" is the most common word used to describe the Long Barn experience.

LEFT *While this elegant armoire from Lark Vintage was likely previously placed in a much different setting, here it sets a beautiful tone. It came in multiple parts, so it was another test of patience to reassemble, but so worth the effort. A moment of faded grandeur among the minimalist decor brings a romantic touch to functional storage.*

ABOVE *Two white wood slatted doors, one leading to a loo and one to the washer and dryer. The delightful tiny window offers a massive view.*
RIGHT *I found seven scalloped marble tiles some time ago, and they had the perfect rustic and bohemian flair for this small bathroom.*

OVERLEAF *Artisan white square tiles and mosaic marble flooring are offset by a pop of vibrant turquoise from the towel rack (left). A nod to my signature floral affair in the form of a metal wall hook, which displays a crocheted voile nightdress (right).*

THE OLD SCHOOL HOUSE

A WORLD OF MAKE-BELIEVE

Rumor has it, and I choose to believe, that this building was the original school for the local village. It would have been accessed by the local children, perhaps via horse and cart, through a gate from the street into my walled garden.

How I love this structure! It reminds me of my Prairie days in Texas. While it is most definitely in need of repair, which would be an expensive and time-consuming undertaking, I lavish much love and gratitude on this old building precisely for all its imperfections and fragilities. Inside, the walls are a mish-mash of finishes: raw stone, brick and plaster, which over the years has taken on the most magical patina of pinks and greens.

The roof is made of corrugated tin, the standard for farm outbuildings, which brings me so much joy especially on a windy rainy day. While protected inside, the sounds of the weather are amplified, dramatic and raw. The wooden slatted double door is one of three entrances; the opening mechanism is a primitive screw system that some would find tedious, but I rather like.

Heavenly light streams in from the different openings, through the cracks and brokenness of walls and roof, only made possible by hundreds of years of wear and crumbling. Even on a cold, dark day, the light is magical. I spend a lot of time in this tranquil and calm space, which has become the perfect backdrop for the storytelling of Shabby Chic.

The Old School House is home to many of my props gathered over the years from all over the world, as well as other treasures new and old. Whenever I enter, there is always a moment of theater ready for storytelling.

RIGHT *When the large, wonky wooden doors are open, this old school house/barn is a breathtaking sight, illuminated by beautiful light. A few of my treasures that crossed the pond from the US didn't find a home in the main house, but they have not been abandoned. They are valued, protected and loved here in this resourceful space, which is used primarily for photo shoots in the many worlds of Shabby Chic. Hanging but not abandoned, these timeworn chandeliers await restoration, ready for re-loving.*

OVERLEAF *The sign that hung over the shop at The Prairie is taking a pause—I dream that one day it will have a new life (left). A beautiful bucket of flowers and a bright-blue velvet sofa, captured in whimsical light along with me (right).*

SHABBY CHIC Couture
HOLY

ABOVE *Over the span of 36 years, there have been many labels for my multiple brands. This linen roll from Rachel Ashwell Couture is one of my favorites.* **RIGHT** *A simply gorgeous chunkily carved lamp with fading painted flowers stands alongside my extensive collection of interesting and intricate lampshades, all flea-market finds.*

OVERLEAF *I treasure my faux flowers: they have satisfied many celebrations, especially during hot summer days when real flowers would struggle to remain fresh under the hot sun (left). The steel-framed windows are an industrial moment against the patina of plaster and stone walls (right). A "bespoke" sign has been retrieved for later use.*

BESPOKE

LEFT *An exquisite gift from the talented Grace Barzyz, a true master artist with all forms of vintage paper. Fine tissue paper, wallpaper and trims create what I call my Tissue Tutus.*

ABOVE *A multicolored twinkly chandelier and a distressed white-painted metal beauty with floral details are reproductions from my lighting collection at Next, inspired by vintage finds.*

TREASURE HUNTING

Much of Meadow Manor is furnished with flea-market finds gathered patiently from my travels in both the US and the UK. I have been going to flea markets my whole life. I was first introduced to the experience by my parents as a young girl, as searching for treasures was at the core of both their businesses: my dad looking for first-edition books, my mum for vintage dolls and bits of silk, ribbons and lace to make and restore their dresses. I didn't realize it at the time, but following her around and observing how she layered priceless silks with slightly tattered ribbons and laces gave me my first lessons in shabby and chic.

I love everything about flea markets: the excitement of the unknown waiting to be discovered and the exchange of stories shared as each purchase is considered. There is so much satisfaction in finding soulful, one-of-a-kind pieces that display the workmanship of days gone by. Vintage items have their own beauty, offering patinas and finishes that have taken years in the making. The imperfections, sometimes minor and hidden, are evidence of a life lived and loved.

I am always searching for textiles, often finding once brightly colored florals that have been bleached by the sun and faded to a smokier palette over time. I appreciate every treasure I choose to buy. Sometimes they are my forever-to-keep, sometimes for a gift, sometimes they are inspiration for my design work or part of the thread of a tapestry in my storytelling. For me, the discovering and acquiring is often enough, and without attachment it is joyful for me to pass on.

When decorating with vintage, I am always mindful to leave space for each piece to have room to be celebrated and seen. I believe the area around it should be clean and uncluttered, but not sterile, to better embrace the warmth of these treasures. It takes vision to imagine a found object in the right context and placement, where its unique qualities and captivating presence reveal its priceless value. As the saying goes, one man's junk is another man's treasure. When a piece becomes your discovered treasure, there is a special moment within of poetry and grace.

RIGHT *George and I on a flea-market escapade. In our excitement I forgot to bring his leash, so a vendor gave me a bit of rope. He always waits so patiently when I find a treasure to consider, often conversing with the multitude of other pups that frequent the markets.*

HUILE

WIDE-OPEN SPACES

AND A MAJESTIC CLUSTER OF TEMPLE BARNS

In the wide-open spaces that surround Meadow Manor, the physical beauty of home meets the spiritual essence of the land. The unobstructed views of the rolling hills are pure peace, interrupted at times by the seasonal panorama of harvesting by way of tractors and meandering cows, deer and birds sweeping from field to field. Time has stood still here. Having nothing but nature to rest one's eyes upon inspires meaningful thought, sometimes simply gratitude or a clearing of the mind to be quiet and still; the slowing down of life.

While Meadow Manor has a graceful grandeur, it is surrounded by a cluster of old outbuildings, timeworn but still standing. They are evidence of the days when all was a working farm. A cluster of barns facing the open landscape is unrestored and ready for re-loving. I have named this group the Temple Barns, as even in their present state of decay, with their wonky rooflines, they have a sense of the spiritual. I respect and appreciate their poise and strength of character, alongside their vulnerability.

The Temple Barns are bleached from the sun and rusty from the rain, not to mention cracked, warped and bruised from centuries of sheltering hard labor and weathering storms. My dream would one day be to renovate these barns and create a destination for creative people to congregate: musicians, poets, writers and artists alike. I experience glimpses of this by way of many of my friends and family passing through and finding inspiration and community here.

Unlike a tended garden with considered planting—in my case it would have to be pastel blooms and anything fluffy—wide-open spaces have the freedom to be wild. At times the offerings are wildflowers or billowing long grasses, all beautiful in their seasonal colors. Letting nature choose her expression is an important reminder of impermanence, of letting things be. And it's always perfect.

RIGHT *Wandering through the long golden grass with vistas of the rambling, rolling Somerset hills is very different from my California life of wide sandy Malibu beaches where the ocean meets the sky. Both scenes are intoxicating and calming—the gift of nature that keeps giving.*

OVERLEAF *The grasses in the meadow behind the Long Barn can grow above 4ft/1.2m before trimming is needed. It's my favorite time in nature's cycle, when the breeze creates a gentle mesmerizing wave. The rooflines of the Temple Barns are simply delightful, with old clay tiles, timeworn corrugated metal, blond stone and weathered wood—the most beautiful backdrop for my vintage Sanderson armchair (pages 188 and 189). No matter where, George believes any chair is placed solely for him, so he sits proud and entitled.*

SINCLAIR MELSON LTD
BY APPOINTMENT TO
HER MAJESTY THE QUEEN
UPHOLSTERERS

I love to wander through the fields when the grasses become unruly and tall. I create pathways for ease of movement, as often I am not empty-handed.

ABOVE AND RIGHT *This barn would make a lovely cottage conversion, retaining as many of its original features as possible both inside and out. But until such time, I use it endlessly and love to capture moments here of whimsy and surprise.*

OVERLEAF *This columned arch has hosted weddings at The Prairie in Texas, which has similar wide-open countryside views. Now put back together after being taken apart for the journey, it pauses here before it is put back to work in the pasture.*

MY NEIGHBORHOOD

THE TAPESTRY OF MY COUNTRY LIVING

Making a move to a new country can be daunting. Even though I was returning to my homeland of 40 years ago, it was London I had left, with little experience of country living. I pushed away fears and insecurities surrounding such a decision, but I was mindful to consider the makeup of the communities I visited during my three years of renting the farm cottage that was to be my stepping stone into fully embracing English rural life.

I would often go to a Sunday service at local churches to mingle with the congregation, wander around the streets and pop into the pubs and shops, all to try and get a sense of the lives being lived there. When thinking about my future home in the countryside, it was important to find a community with the right balance of friendliness, kindness and connection without being too cliquey. The notion of being able to walk to a corner shop was also high up on my list.

My little neighborhood checked all the boxes. It lies above the Mells River in the Mendip Hills, surrounded by ancient woodland. I am able to walk George along the river to my local shop and pub, come rain or shine. English manners are a real thing: people are kind and friendly, and there is a grounded sense of community. Some families have lived in the neighborhood for generations, while others like myself have made the conscious choice to settle in the countryside to slow down, be inspired and find a new lease of life.

There is a strong cultural history here, too. Back in the day, owners of the grander manors in the neighborhood attracted artists, poets, politicians and society folk who left their mark, giving the area a lasting creative legacy. All said, my little slice of Somerset is an inspiring environment. I am meeting people who are curious and productive at a pace that suits them, outside the fast lane, while still very much involved in living.

RIGHT *A lovely mile or so walk from my house along the river is my local pub, The Talbot Inn. The entrance is through a historic carriage arch where once upon a time top-hatted coachmen and tired, muddy horses rattled through, pulling large creaking coaches piled high with travelers and luggage. The arch leads through to a cobbled courtyard and the old stables, now a succession of country dining areas.*

OVERLEAF *I simply adore these little country village streets. It's as though time has stood still, both due to the timeless stone cottages with hollyhocks and roses round the doors, but also the slow meandering strolls that are a part of daily life.*

THE TALBOT INN
THE TALBOT INN

THE
TALBOT
INN

THE TALBOT INN
MY LOCAL PUB

Buildings round here tend to have history and The Talbot Inn, a blessing to have within walking distance, is no exception. Established way back in 1480 and rebuilt here and there over the years, it is a quintessential English countryside inn and pub. The sign on The Talbot Inn is an elegantly poised medieval hunting dog, and can be spotted on the approach from the charming English country road.

Nowadays, locals and visitors enter through a historic carriage arch. While jolly, the place is never rowdy, which isn't always the case with English pub culture. The Talbot reminds me of the pub in the movie *The Holiday*, romantic and timeless, and there's a skittle alley, a must-have English pub activity. George enjoys meeting up with other dogs, who are always welcome, nestled under the tables waiting for leftovers or close by one of the many roaring fireplaces.

During the winter months of cold, rainy or snowy days the fireplaces and candles make the wood-paneled interior picture-book cosy, while during the warmer months, the cobbled courtyard and garden are a sea of summer frocks.

When I have family and friends staying, it has become a tradition to walk along the river, past the post office and corner shop, and then along a charming stretch of cottages to The Talbot Inn. My drink of choice is elderflower spritzer, as I've never been drawn to alcohol, and the fish and chips are my favorite dish on the menu. I am always grateful for these simple pleasures.

LEFT *The weather in England is very fickle—a clear blue sky can quickly be overtaken by clouds and rain. However, when the sun is out, even briefly, outdoor pub life is appreciated and thoroughly enjoyed.*

OVERLEAF *At this gastropub there are multiple rooms and cosy nooks for locals and for visitors from far and wide, enjoying the great food and staying in the comfortable bedrooms (left). English pubs are typically dark and cosy, and while I've never had a pint of beer, the smell is familiar and nostalgic. Amy Neunsinger, who photographed this book, also has a range of candles named La Rouge. We snuck one in, along with some of my dinnerware staples, to create a shabby and chic moment (right).*

My local church dates back to the 12th century; it is teeny and humble, but supports a very active congregation. I'm not a regular, but the Christmas carol service feels like stepping back in time into a classic storybook or movie. I don't consider myself religious, but more spiritual. I strive to stay connected with myself and my life on a soul level and follow my heart to guide me to make good and kind choices.

THE WALLED GARDEN AT MELLS
AN ABUNDANCE OF BEAUTY

Just down the road from The Talbot Inn is the enchanting Walled Garden at Mells. I love it so, this rambling piece of paradise nestled in the pastoral hills. It is an ancient space. The bones of the garden are from the 15th century, and the honey-colored walls, still covered in ancient fixings for fruit trees and vines, were put up during the 17th century.

Sometimes I visit the garden taking my guests, but at other times I pop in by myself. In between my stream of visitors, I can easily take on the role of a hermit. But when I feel the pull of companionship, a meandering walk along the river leads me to a gentle talk with the current custodians, Cosmo Fry and Diane Birch, who have become friends of mine. We talk about their passion for flowers and their plans for this sacred property. Diane is a singer-songwriter and has shared with me that she is often inspired to write lyrics that draw from the beautiful library of floral names. Having them and this secret garden on my doorstep is priceless to me.

The Walled Garden is a whimsical space with the yummiest café selling locally baked goods and pizzas made in their own oven. There's a garden shop, too, with an enviable stock of roses and other plants. One of the things that make this garden so special is the view over ancient meadows on its south side, so you experience all those walled-garden sensations of protection and shelter without feeling closed in.

Cosmo and Diane are, in their own words, committed to honoring the legacy of this place and continuing to unfold its abundant beauty. They are simply building on what's already there, looking and listening to the landscape and slowly threading their own vision and imagination through it. They intend to keep their gardens chemical free while growing vibrant perennials and wildflowers, many grown from seed, as well as an abundance of roses, both classics and rare varieties. On summer evenings, there will be music, but more English chamber music than rock and roll.

I haven't yet tackled my own walled garden, nor the lawn and the surrounding areas, as I need to learn and understand the English countryside rhythm of what plants are conducive to the climate and the soil. Each time I set foot in The Walled Garden, even just while waiting for my oven-baked pizza, I leave with more knowledge of plants. I also take inspiration from Cosmo's genius restoration of walls, secret uncovered doorways and fences and the different structures he makes from tree trunks and branches, which are inconspicuous yet exquisite. There is so much food for thought here, and so many ideas that one day I can carry back to Meadow Manor.

RIGHT *I am on a journey of learning about English country gardens. Little by little, I will one day implement my lessons in my own garden. Often after walking George, I will pop into the Walled Garden at Mells. While I'm not ready to buy plants yet, I'm learning the local offerings so that when I'm ready I will have a place to begin.*

OVERLEAF *My new friends Cosmo and Diane, the owners of the Walled Garden, are generous with their wisdom. They are a massive source of inspiration in the way they design the nursery. It is a sacred world filled with plants, flowers and unobtrusive but impressive structures, including this spectacular pergola and dining table built by Cosmo—perfect for communal dining or large parties.*

ABOVE *A magical, whimsical and sacred entryway into the Walled Garden, a sanctuary for a world of curated nature.*
RIGHT *Looking into the Rose Terrace, where ancient views unfurl.*
OVERLEAF *Ancient doors in ancient walls, promising surprises and enclosing secret places (left and right). A large greenhouse also serves as an indoor dining area on a chilly or rainy day, sharing space with grapevines and geraniums (pages 214–215). There is a lovely sense of community here. Rarely do I pop by and not see a familiar face, and the collective environment of all that is here is heartwarming and peaceful to experience.*

WHIMSICAL GARDENS

FLOWERS FOR THOUGHT

For the past couple of years, I've been focusing on making Meadow Manor a home and I have not given much thought to the gardens. My house has a sweeping front lawn and a walled garden to the side and is surrounded by pastures, meadows and an orchard over yonder. The previous owners were ardent gardeners and they did most everything themselves with little outside help. I haven't had the bandwidth or knowledge to consider the outside spaces other than to plant a dahlia cutting bed and some jasmine, but I have been mindful to maintain what was already there. Coming from California, I am used to irrigation and plenty of sun, both scarcities at Meadow Manor, so in the summer months I've become well acquainted with my hose. Similar to my laundry practice, I have reframed the chore of watering my garden at sunset as a walking meditation. It often keeps me outdoors late into the night, when I may be tired, but it's a soulful way to end the day and inspires me to feel connected to the roses, lavender and other plants I have inherited. In the meantime, I am gathering knowledge and inspiration of how to design and evolve the gardens of Meadow Manor.

LIBBY'S GARDEN
THE CRÈME DE LA CRÈME

Libby Russell is a landscape designer and plantswoman with over 25 years of experience all over the world. I came across her magic land on an open house garden tour. She has created a breathtaking experience, two decades in the making. The property is grand and the grounds are vast, so Libby has cleverly created many standalone garden areas, from rolling lawns to stunningly organized but not manicured borders, climbing roses and bushes of beauty. The gardens tell multiple glorious stories with a common thread of Libby's touch throughout, merging together into a masterpiece. Each time I visit the garden, there are more and more takeaways of precious and curated big and little worlds to scribble in my notebook. Libby is generous in her knowledge and advice on where and how to begin the beautiful journey. She is a master of her craft and passionate, which is an inspiration in itself. Nature and conditions cannot be controlled, but Libby has managed to find consistency in creating the enthralling beauty that she shares with the world.

RIGHT *I have visited Libby Russell's magnificent garden a few times, and it is simply beautiful. While her gardens are 20 years in the making, I can but dream. However, I am gathering knowledge of what is possible and appropriate for an English country garden. The cascading greenery over the secret gate is on my vision board, providing inspiration for my stone arches and entryways.*

OVERLEAF *While the cluster of Libby's structures is very different from mine, I've taken note that she has created a center within to give a sense of whole. The borders have their own individuality, not matchy-matchy but cohesive. I have a very similar wall to this rose-clad beauty, so this dream is achievable, given patience* *(pages 220–221).*

ABOVE *A humble rustic moment that resonates with me.*
RIGHT *A swimming pool is not on my agenda, but if it was, this is what I would visualize.*

OVERLEAF *While I am not so good at remembering specific names of flowers outside of roses, peonies, dahlias, lisianthus and sweet peas, this symphony of flowers is everything I love.*

BELLE'S BEAUTY
THE QUINTESSENTIAL ENGLISH COTTAGE GARDEN

Belle's garden is everything my heart desires. It is quite a tiny space that she and her mum Amanda have cultivated. They are the sole carers of this precious garden and familiar with every square inch. The property is positioned with views of rambling hills, adding to the illusion of size, but once you are nestled in the grounds, it is intimate, enchanting and breathtaking.

There are places to sit and eat in the sun and shade, a moment to snooze in the hammock, veggies for all and seeds propagating in the greenhouse, as well as showstopping performances of roses and sweet peas.

Belle's love of faded floral fabrics creates a timeless backdrop for the garden flowers. Standing still, every glance is rewarded with a flower. I am endlessly inspired by the consistency of palette—pastels, of course—as well as the carefully considered placement in this small setting, so that the vast variety of florals cohabit with abundance while leaving room for each to have its own space.

I often think of my mum's petite garden. She always had an outdoor space that she could personally take care of, so she could be intimately involved with every petal. I believe in that philosophy wholeheartedly, but it's not remotely possible in the case of Meadow Manor. But I do want to be sure to go slow; to learn and make choices so the end result reflects my vision and me—a mix of simple and fancy.

I hope in time to take to Meadow Manor all that inspires me from these gardens, but I know it starts with feeling fully connected to the process of each and every decision. I look forward to the day when the outdoor spaces are as much a home as the interiors I have created.

RIGHT *A sun-bleached floral parasol by Staycation Vintage creates an intimate setting for many a cup of tea I have enjoyed in this fairy-tale floral garden.*

OVERLEAF *Every inch of this garden is thoughtfully planted with roses of all varieties along with other feminine and romantic flowers. Swaying in the hammock among the florals is a dream unto itself.*

LEFT *The storybook cottage that the garden surrounds is pretty and petite. During the warmer days the veranda is a well-used space, decorated with floral fabrics and vintage finds.*
ABOVE *The little fairy-like flowers on the stone steps caught my eye for the gems they are.*

OVERLEAF *The bluey-pink shades of David Austin roses are my favorite (left and right). Belle and Amanda take care of every plant, petal and weed on the property. It's a labor of love. Food for thought for my future garden, but in the meantime, I am a welcomed guest with notebook in hand.*

RESOURCES

Rachel Ashwell Shabby Chic
www.shabbychic.com
@officialshabbychic
@rachelashwell

Shabby Chic by Rachel Ashwell
www.next.co.uk

ARTISTS AND MAKERS

Angela Fleming
www.egsewingstudio.com
@emmalinesgarden

Ben Peck-Whiston
www.benpeckwhiston.com
@benpeckwhiston

Grace Barzyz
@gracebarzyz

Jorunn Mulen
www.jorunn-mulen.com
@jorunnmulen

Laurence Amelie
www.laurence-amelie.com
@gallery.laurence.amelie

Lily Ashwell
www.lilyashwell.com
@lilyashwell

Staycation Vintage Parasols
www.staycationvintageparasols.com
@staycationvintageparasols

WALLS AND FLOORS

Bert & May
www.bertandmay.com
@bertandmay

Farrow & Ball
www.farrow-ball.com
@farrowandball

Fired Earth
www.firedearth.com
@firedearthuk

Francesca's Paints
www.francescaspaint.com
@francescaspaintsltd

Original Style
www.originalstyle.com
@originalstyleuk

Starel Stones
www.starelstones.co.uk
@starel_stones

KITCHENS, BATHROOMS AND STOVES

Bertazzoni
uk.bertazzoni.com
@bertazzoni_official

Burlington
www.burlingtonbathrooms.com
@burlingtonbathroom

Cast Iron Bath Company
www.castironbath.co.uk
@castironbathcompany

Charnwood
www.charnwood.com
@charnwoodstoves

deVOL
www.devolkitchens.co.uk
@devolkitchens

VINTAGE AND PRELOVED

Etsy
www.etsy.com

Frome Reclamation
www.fromerec.co.uk
@frome.rec

Lark Vintage
www.larkvintage.co.uk
@larkvintage

The Original Round Top Antiques Fair
www.roundtoptexasantiques.com
@roundtopantiquestexas

The Frome Independent
thefromeindependent.org.uk
@thefromeindependent

The Giant Shepton Flea Market
www.sheptonflea.com
@sheptonflea

FABRICS AND TEXTILES

Bennison
www.bennisonfabrics.com

The Curtain Exchange
www.thecurtainexchange.co.uk
@thecurtainexchange_

FLOWERS AND FRAGRANCE

La Rouge Candle
www.larougecandle.com
@la_rouge_candle

Toria Britten
www.wildlybeautiful.co.uk
@wildlybeautifulflowers

Victoria Sheppard
@the_witham_flowery

BUSINESS CREDITS

Belle Daughtry
www.justbelle.co.uk
@just_belle

Amanda Daughtry
@mysimplehome
The garden of photographer and stylist Belle Daughtry and her mother Amanda (pages 226–233).

Libby Russell
www.mazzullorussell
landscapedesign.com
The garden of landscape designer Libby Russell (pages 216–225).

The Talbot Inn
www.talbotinn.com
The Talbot Inn in Mells, Somerset (pages 197–203).

The Walled Garden at Mells
www.thewalledgardenatmells.co.uk
The Walled Garden at Mells in Somerset, owned by Cosmo Fry and Diane Birch (pages 206–215).

FREE HAND FLORALS
HANDCUT STENCILS
BEN PECK WHISTON
TILES
BLAKE + BULL
ENAMEL
COLORS
ELECTRIC
CONVERSION
FIRED EARTH
BERT + MAY
ORIGINAL STYLE

INDEX

Page numbers in *italic* refer to the illustrations and their captions

ACKNOWLEDGMENTS

Maintaining established roots in the US while setting new roots in the UK is a privilege and has proved exciting as well as wonky at times. Life and how to find balance continues to unfold. I consider myself a storyteller—sometimes the lines blur from dream to reality, and Meadow Manor at times feels like a dream. I hope this book captures that dream.

Thank you to all who have supported me on this Meadow Manor journey and whatever the future holds.

To Lily and Jake for being home to me, wherever we are, together or apart.

To my stepdaughter Eve and husband Charlie, thank you for loving Meadow Manor and for the love you gift to me.

To my forever friends in the US, who hold space for me as I live within two worlds and reconnect seamlessly with me when our paths cross.

To my new friends in Somerset for welcoming me into your lives with open arms.

To Ben and David Peck-Whiston for caring for Meadow Manor as though it was your own.

To Diana for making my first home, my rental cottage on your farm, my safe space from which to explore and build this new chapter, and in doing so creating the most heartwarming memories.

To my publisher CICO Books as well as Alex and Geoff. This is our fifth book together—you know me and my worlds so well and support my vision to completion.

To Amy Neunsinger, for capturing what my eyes see and my heart feels.

And lastly to George, for making Meadow Manor a home.

VINTAGE
FURNITURE
This vintage furniture was personally chosen for their unique design, coloration, and character. Each has a beauty, uniqueness, and variation all its own. Please handle with gentle care.
Kindness is
a lot of things
13 11 95